AF408407

Happy In Your Skin
Is Rafa Different

Erlin Kakkana

THIS BOOK IS DEDICATED TO MY CHILDREN

THANK YOU FOR GIVING ME THE
OPPORTUNITY TO BE THE BEST MOM!

MY SPOUSE WHO SUPPORTS ME IN ALL MY
ENDEAVORS AS A MOM, FRIEND, AND
PARTNER

WE ARE THE BOOKS WE READ AND THE
THINGS WE LOVE.

- CATH CROWLEY

This book belongs to

____

Rafa loved his family,
His grandma, mom, and dad.

He loved his sister, and
The fun times that they had!

His family, from India,
Now lived in the Midwest.

It was the USA,
And really was the best!

But sometimes Rafa got
questions from his friends.

Like, "Why is your skin brown?"
It made Rafa feel strange.

At first, he didn't like
to talk about his looks.

He'd rather sit and read
one of his new books.

One day Rafa went
for his annual health check.

Rafa was surprised!
Rafa noticed doctor Patel's skin.

Guess what? She was brown!
She was just like him.

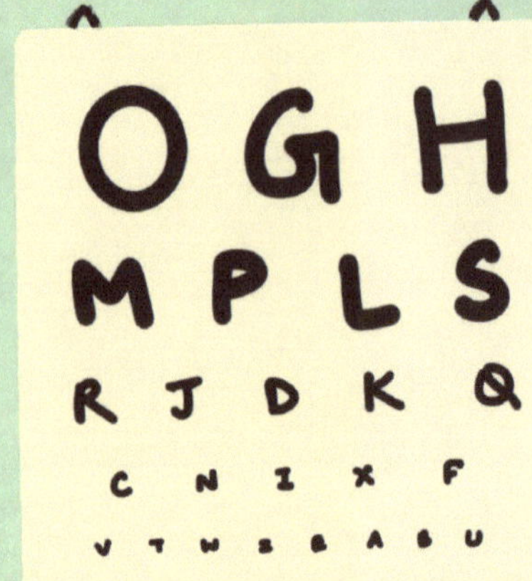

But he was curious and
so Rafa gathers his thoughts and asks:

"Do people ever ask,
about your skin color, Doctor?"

Doctor Patel smiled.
"Yes, sometimes people have questions"

She gave some advice,
And he went on his way.

Next time someone asked...
He'd know what to say!

When Rafa started school
and went to his new class,

He saw his new teacher,
It quickly made him gasp.

Mr. Joshi looked like him

Rafa was excited
and so Rafa asked
his teacher if he got
questions about his color.

"It is not as much,
as they were before!
It did make me sad,
But no, not anymore!"

Mr. Joshi then shares a way
Rafa could respond.
Rafa liked his teacher.
They had a special bond.

That day when Rafa went home after school

Rafa's dad said
"Your teacher left a message,"

"We heard about the questions,
That you get from your friends."

They sat Rafa down and explained the proud culture and history of Asian Indians.

Rafa's mom and dad gave him things to say,
When questions about his appearance,
color and ethnicity were asked!

So, when Tina said,
"Why's your skin color different than mine?"

Rafa looked up, smiled, and said
"I was born this way,"

That's one way Dr. Patel told Rafa he could say.

When Rafa was at the gym that day,

"Why are you so different?"
Someone asked.

Rafa then remembered,
What Mom had said to him.

"Our uniqueness and difference make the world,
A much prettier place."

Rafa felt so proud to embrace his authentic self
And share it with his friends.

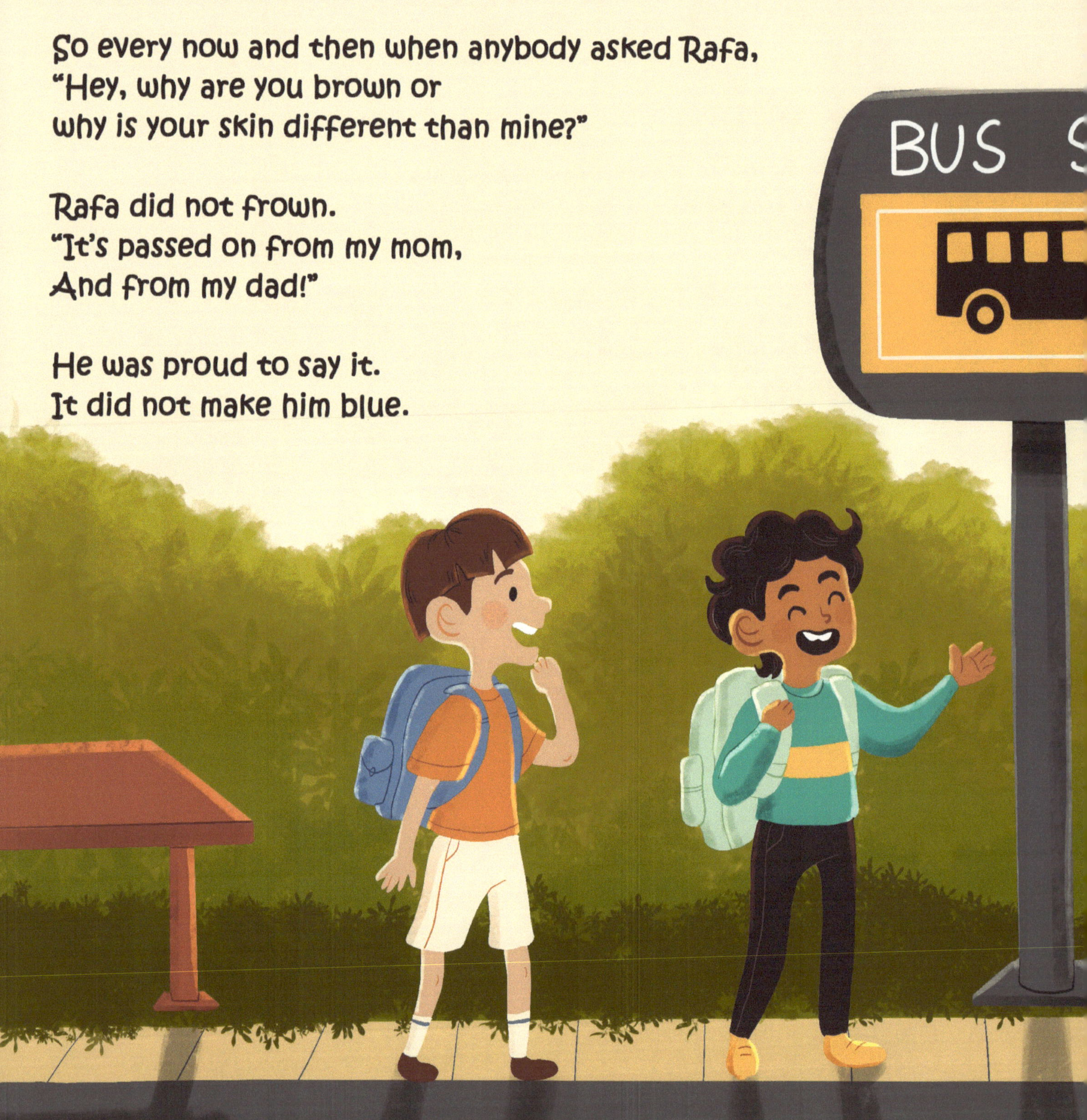

So every now and then when anybody asked Rafa,
"Hey, why are you brown or
why is your skin different than mine?"

Rafa did not frown.
"It's passed on from my mom,
And from my dad!"

He was proud to say it.
It did not make him blue.

Rafa's doctor taught him the importance
to love and appreciate one's own self.

His parents helped him to
Be proud of who he was.

His teacher showed Rafa that he can be anything
And always to be happy in his skin.

Maybe Rafa was different..
But he was proud to be himself

And embracing his differences and uniqueness
Makes the world a prettier place and

For Rafa
That was a win!

The End

India is a country in South Asia.

It is the seventh-largest country by area,

and the second-most populous country

The Peacock is the national bird of India and symbolizes grace and beauty.

Dance forms are an important aspect of the Indian art and culture,

Bharatnatyam is the oldest dance form in India

We hope you enjoyed this story and we would love to see your ongoing support for our upcoming titles about how Rafa explores and learns about his ethnicity and cultural identity.

Rafa's family helps Rafa understand and appreciate his differences and uniqueness and build on his strengths.

ERLIN KAKKANAD - Author

Thank you for making my book a part
of your family and supporting my work.

I am passionate about bringing awareness to
cultural and ethnic diversity through stories from
my lived experience in India and USA.

Through my books, I intend to help our future
leaders build on their social-cultural skills which
are key to becoming inclusive members of our
community and great (future) leaders!

Please send in feedback here:
erlinkakkanad@gmail.com

Testimonials and reviews go a long way
for authors in the self-publishing world.

And thank you for doing your bit.
Your review and testimonial mean a lot
to me!

Leave a review on Amazon today!

I look forward to hearing from you!

New titles are coming soon:

Rafa navigates his lunch room experience in Kindergarten
I love curry and I'm not sorry

Connect with the author and give us a follow on Instagram
@Erlin_KidscareShare

www.ingramcontent.com/pod-product-compliance
Lightning Source LLC
Chambersburg PA
CBHW042023110726

48010CB00007B/219